**BBC earth**

DO YOU KNOW?

Level 4

LOOKING AFTER THE OCEAN

Inspired by BBC Earth TV series and developed with input from BBC Earth natural history specialists

Written by Ruth A. Musgrave
Text adapted by Hannah Fish
Series Editor: Nick Coates

LADYBIRD BOOKS

UK | USA | Canada | Ireland | Australia
India | New Zealand | South Africa

Ladybird Books is part of the Penguin Random House group of companies
whose addresses can be found at global.penguinrandomhouse.com.
www.penguin.co.uk   www.puffin.co.uk   www.ladybird.co.uk

First published 2020
001

Contents

New words

air

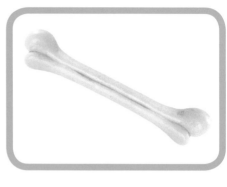

bone

heat
(noun)

hunt
(verb)

lay eggs

medicine

plastic
(adjective and noun)

pollution

protect

recycle

scientist

seaweed

How many oceans are there?

Ocean water is always moving. It moves up and down, and it travels around the Earth.

There is only one ocean. People use names for different parts of the ocean: Pacific Ocean, Atlantic Ocean, Arctic Ocean, Southern Ocean and Indian Ocean.

Atlantic Ocean

Pacific Ocean

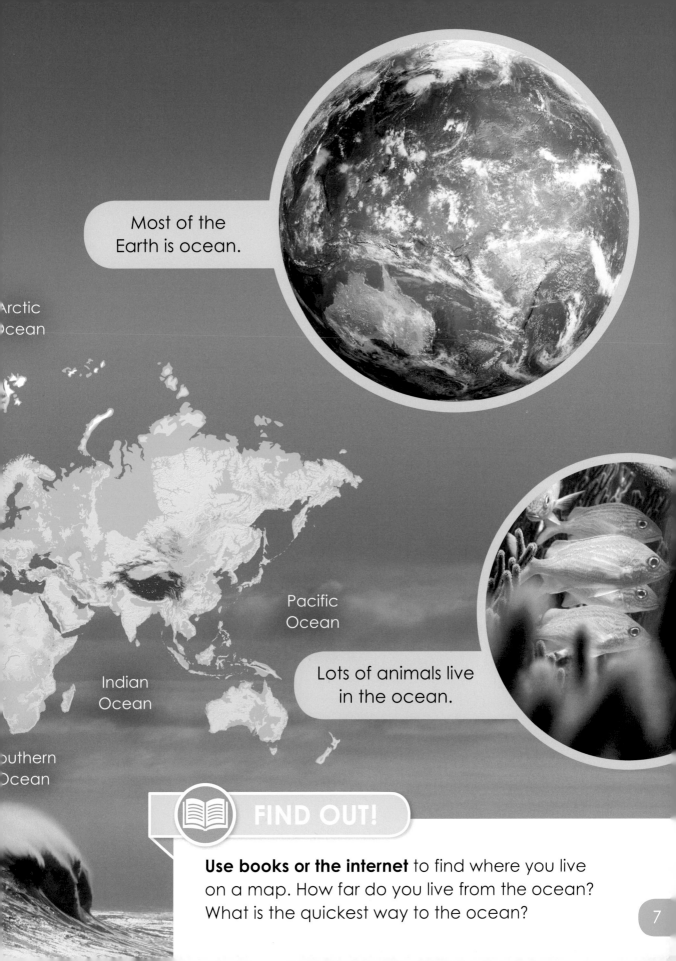

Most of the Earth is ocean.

Arctic Ocean

Pacific Ocean

Indian Ocean

Lots of animals live in the ocean.

Southern Ocean

FIND OUT!

Use books or the internet to find where you live on a map. How far do you live from the ocean? What is the quickest way to the ocean?

Why is the ocean important?

The ocean is very important for the Earth's weather.

The **heat** from the sun goes into the ocean. Ocean water moves the heat around the Earth. This helps different parts of the Earth to get warmer or colder.

The ocean helps to make the **air** around us. **Seaweed** and other ocean plants make oxygen. This is a part of air. We need oxygen to live.

People make **medicines** from ocean plants and animals.

We need the ocean for food. We eat many animals and plants that live there.

LOOK!

Look at the pages.
How do we use ocean plants?

What lives in the ocean?

Many interesting animals and plants live in the ocean. Every day, **scientists** find new ocean animals and plants.

The blue whale is the biggest animal on Earth. Some blue whales are longer than two school buses!

Coral reefs are homes for many animals.

Jellyfish have no **bones** or eyes! They catch fish with their long tentacles.

tentacle

In the Arctic, walruses sleep on the ice.

Sea otters and seals find food in seaweed forests.

seal

THINK!

Some seaweed can grow about 60 centimetres a day. If you started to grow that fast, how much taller would you be after a week?

Who changes the ocean?

The places where animals live are called habitats.

Usually, animal habitats change very slowly. It can take millions of years. Plants and animals also change slowly to live in these habitats. But people change these habitats quickly.

Baby turtles are born on the beach. But people have changed the turtles' habitat. This is difficult for the turtles.

People build cities, towns and roads in animal habitats, so the animals may need to move to new habitats.

People make **pollution**. Rivers and rain carry pollution to the ocean.

You can find pollution from all over the world across the ocean. The pollution is changing the ocean.

WATCH!

Watch the video (see page 32).
How have people changed the baby turtles' habitat?
What makes the turtles go the wrong way?
Where do they go?

Why do we study the ocean?

Many scientists study the ocean. We need to understand more about the ocean. This will help us to **protect** it.

Ships take scientists far out into the ocean.

There are many ways
to study the ocean.

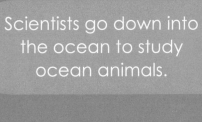

Scientists go down into
the ocean to study
ocean animals.

This scientist is studying
a whale shark.

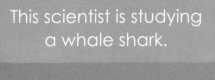

A six-gilled shark looks at the
scientists in the deep ocean.

THINK!

People have only studied a small part of the ocean.
Why do you think people haven't studied more?

What's that noise?

Ocean animals need to make and hear sounds.

Scientists want to know more about how ocean animals use and make sounds.

Scientists listen to the clownfish. Clownfish make a lot of noise!

People make a lot of noise in the ocean. This is called noise pollution.

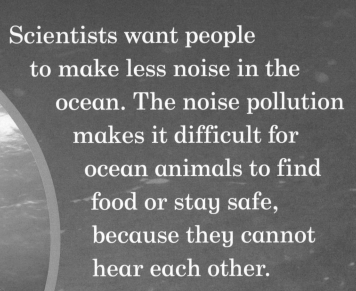

Scientists want people to make less noise in the ocean. The noise pollution makes it difficult for ocean animals to find food or stay safe, because they cannot hear each other.

Many animals, like dolphins, use sounds to help them travel around the ocean.

Clownfish listen to each other. Their noises tell other clownfish if something dangerous is near.

WATCH!

Watch the video (see page 32).
What do the clownfish do when the scientist puts a dangerous animal next to them?
Why is it important that we understand clownfish?

How do people help sea turtles?

Every year, when they are ready to **lay their eggs**, sea turtles climb on to the beach. In the past, people ate the eggs and **hunted** the turtles. But now, some people look after turtles.

People in this village protect the leatherback turtles' beaches.

The people move the eggs if they are too near to the water.

They teach children about the turtles.

Twenty years ago, only 30 or 40 leatherback turtles came on to the beach each night to lay their eggs. Now, more than 500 turtles come on to the beach to lay their eggs.

PROJECT

Work in a group.
How many different kinds of sea turtles are there? Use books or the internet to find out. Make a list of all the different ones you find. Draw a picture of your favourite turtle.

What happened to all the herrings?

Many years ago, people did not think about how many fish they caught. Every year, they took lots of herrings from the ocean.

Then, the animals and people did not have enough herrings in the ocean to eat.

To help protect the fish, people stopped taking lots of herrings. The number of herrings began to grow. Now there are many herrings in the ocean.

People and animals catch herrings to eat.

Humpback whales and orcas eat herrings.

Seabirds take herrings from the ocean.

KILDIN

KILDIN

F·66·BD

PETREL

🔍 LOOK!

Look at the pages.
What happened to the number of herrings when people took fewer fish?

Where did that shark go?

Scientists want to know where whale sharks have their babies. This will help them to protect the sharks.

net

Sometimes whale sharks swim into fishing nets and cannot get out. If we know where the sharks go, we can stop fishing there.

Whale sharks are the largest fish on Earth. Some are 18 metres long.

This scientist uses a tracking device. It tells him where the mother shark swims.

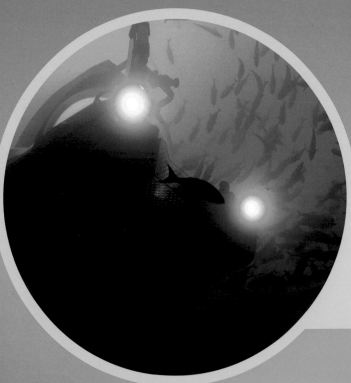

The mother shark swims far under the water. Soon the scientist cannot see her. The tracking device tells the scientist where she is.

WATCH!

Watch the video (see page 32).
How does the scientist get close to the shark?
Where does he put the tracking device?
What does the tracking device show him?

What eats plastic?

Plastic bags, cups, bottles, and other bits of plastic go into the ocean.

This is a dangerous problem for animals all over the world.

This whale has a plastic bag in its mouth.

Many animals think plastic is food. They eat the plastic and not their food.

Scientists are worried about these seabirds. The seabirds think they are giving food to their babies.

But many seabirds are giving plastic to their babies.

We must use less plastic to protect ocean animals. We can also **recycle** old plastic.

PROJECT

Work in a group.
How much plastic do you use in a day? How much plastic do you recycle? Make a list of all the plastics you use.

Can we protect ocean animals?

If people work together, we can keep ocean animals safe.

For hundreds of years, people hunted whales. There were very few humpback whales, grey whales and sperm whales.

In the 1970s and 1980s, people decided to protect whales and stop hunting them.

It is now easy to see a humpback whale jumping out of the sea.

Now, there are more grey whales than in the past.

Large groups of sperm whales swim in the ocean again.

Pollution and fishing are a problem for sharks, sea turtles, seabirds and other ocean animals. Together we can protect them, too.

 **FIND OUT!**

Once, there were almost no grey whales. Now, there are more than in the past. **Use books or the internet** to find out how many grey whales there are.

What can we do?

The world needs the ocean.

The ocean is important for the Earth's weather. The ocean gives the world food. We can help to protect the ocean.

If you eat fish, think about which kind of fish you eat. We must leave some fish in the ocean.

Millions of people need the ocean for food.

We must protect sea turtles, sharks, whales and other ocean animals.

We find pollution and plastic in the ocean every day.

We can recycle paper, glass and plastic.

We can use bags and water bottles again.

 PROJECT

Work in a group.
Make your home and school 'ocean-friendly'.
Look for things that can be recycled or reused.
Write down the different ways you have helped the ocean.

Quiz

Choose the correct answers.

1 The Earth has . . .
   a one ocean with one name.
   b one ocean with five names.
   c five oceans.

2 The biggest animal in the ocean is the . . .
   a blue whale.
   b jellyfish.
   c sea otter.

3 'Habitat' means . . .
   a travelling all over the world.
   b a place where animals live.
   c cities, towns and roads.

4 Which of these sentences is NOT true?
   a Scientists study the ocean.
   b There are many ways to study
     the ocean.
   c Scientists have studied all of the ocean.

5 Clownfish make noises for . . .

   a other clownfish.

   b scientists.

   c dolphins

6 Scientists use tracking devices to . . .

   a stop people fishing.

   b find out where whale sharks go.

   c hunt whale sharks.

7 Plastic in the oceans is . . .

   a food for sea animals.

   b good for sea animals.

   c a problem for sea animals.

8 Which of these sentences is true?

   a There are more grey whales now than in the 1970s.

   b The number of grey whales now is the same as in the 1970s.

   c There are fewer grey whales now than in the 1970s.

BBC earth

Visit **www.ladybirdeducation.co.uk** for
FREE DO YOU KNOW? teaching resources.

- video clips with simplified voiceover and subtitles
- video and comprehension activities
- class projects and lesson plans
- audio recording of every book
- digital version of every book
- full answer keys

To access video clips, audio tracks and digital books:

1 Go to **www.ladybirdeducation.co.uk**
2 Click "Unlock book"
3 Enter the code below

wWcwNNfKXh

Stay safe online! Some of the DO YOU KNOW? activities ask children to do extra research online. Remember:

- ensure an adult is supervising;
- use established search engines such as Google or Kiddle;
- children should never share personal details, such as name, home or school address, telephone number or photos.